LIKE
HAY

LIKE
HAY

Quinton Duval

BEAR STAR PRESS

Bear Star Press
185 Hollow Oak Drive
Cohasset, California 95973
530.891.0360
www.bearstarpress.com

Printed in the United States of America.

Cover art: *Autumn in France* by Emily Carr, 1911.

Author photo: Susan F. Lyon

Cover and book design by Beth Spencer

5   4   3   2

Library of Congress Control Number: 2010919357
ISBN: 978-0-9793745-7-9

The text of this book is set in Warnock Pro on acid-free paper.

The publisher would like to thank Gary Thompson for his considerable assistance with this project.

ACKNOWLEDGMENTS

We thank the editors of the following journals where these poems first appeared:

Art/Life: "Dogwood," "Red Hair," "Washline"

Consumnes River Review: "Watercolor Sketch"

Front Range Review: "Spoon"

Rattlesnake Review: "Morning Letter"

Rockhurst Review: "Early Report"

Also:

Among Summer Pines (chapbook), Rattlesnake Press, 2008: "Man Driving," "Oltremarino," "Geese," "One Bright Morning," "In Memory of Being Happy," "Oceanic," "Red Hair," "The Fabulous Future," "Time's Arrow," "Old Friend," "Morning Tea"

∼

Quinton asked me to help collect, organize, and edit these poems into a collection, and I have done so according to general guidelines we discussed during the last few mornings of his life. *Like Hay* is the result of this effort. I thank Nancy Duval, Sarah Phelan, Sue Lyon, Dennis Schmitz, Paul Zarzyski, Tom Crawford, Beth Spencer, Linda Thompson, Bill Duval, Kathy Kieth, and the Poet's Club (Lisa Dominguez Abraham, Victoria Dalkey, Catherine French, Carol Frith, Susan Kelly-DeWitt, Kathleen Lynch, Mary Zeppa) for their help in this bittersweet labor.

—Gary Thompson

For Nancy, part of everything I see

Foreword

QUINTON DUVAL (1948—2010)

> *The soft release of air,*
> *final vague sound of some word—*
> *what was it going to be—*
> *the secret of the other side?*
>> —from "Like Hay"

Though some of these last poems seem interrupted by death, in the lyrical mix we are almost always *this* side—that was Quinton's gift, to keep us in this world. Poems clear-minded, supple and emotionally right—poems as suppositions, circumstantial but caressing the details—a personal exchange always, colloquial, spare but never forfeiting the thing itself.

Quinton's concerns, early or late in his work, for forty years, his topics, his spiritual geography: back roads of the Sacramento Delta, the small talk of a lover, the heightened answer to life itself, *I've never loved anywhere/ as much as here, with you. I'd do it again/ in a minute. You know me./ I've never had enough* ("Morning Tea"). It's another goodbye poem—he is talking to his wife and beloved Nancy directly, wanting to be clear, never to diminish or lose any part of their relationship, wanting to preserve even the smallest part of the shared past, but also predicating a worthy dying with appropriate rituals—*After breakfast, find Bobo the fisherman/ and his four sons. Tell them to bring rope/ and a sheet of plywood. I've never had/ a ride on plywood.*

Other topics: eating (the poems themselves seem to ripen rather than evolve in their telling), travel (European and local—Quinton liked to be in a car), river scenes, ocean/coastal scenes. A poem's narrative development often depends on scenes sketched briskly by a man who knows what he's looking at ("The Coast at Cley"). The poems in *LIKE HAY* are almost always first-person and inclusive, friendly, the tone in a mellow, lower register, but sometimes ironic and wry because the speaker's at ease with you, charming because he can't help but be charming—*Memory allows their noise to become music...* ("Geese").

Other topics: pictorial art references—Quinton did some art reviews early—("Watercolor Sketch"). And prescient again, death a poet's nagging topic: *The faces in the cancer ward fit/ lives you've known or dreamed"* ("Surprise")—his own quick but difficult dying, the imagined details participated in, *...the doctor's foreign tongue, the voice/ of doom to the seventh power.* But life/death's surprise is also in the lunch the speaker of the poem consents to, the common brown paper bag with the unpromising food he tastes—*surprise/ you like it, goddamn it, you like it.*

His first full-length collection, *Dinner Music* (1984), was Quinton in his late twenties and into his thirties questing, the poems in this collection sometimes discontinuous in the delivery, but the voice enjoying a certain darkness, a "kind of resigned wonder," as William Matthews said of the book—the imagery deliciously strange when the poem finds a less-intense juncture, a connection. You have to love the drama.

Abrupt, startling images— *...blankets spread over the lawn/ as if to bandage it from the hard heels/ of the sun* ("Song of Paraguay")—that are vivid color against the narrative flow. Or, sometimes there is chill realization as the poem goes into the unexplored, the poet identifying with his father, speaking of his father's past in one of the father poems ("My Father Has Told Me")— *...He has not hidden it, but/ lost it, as pieces of himself fell/ into the flesh of his children.* The speaker is one of those pieces. Eventually, in his father's logic, and because the father already knows his own death, the father knows *to the exact hair/ that falls out the instant his soul jerks/ loose from our similar bodies.*

It's a matter-of-fact lyricism, understated, a young poet's often downbeat take on things, like the fish in "The Eyes of Mullet," a bait sack—fish cut up to catch more of themselves— *...in insulting bags like this. Once/ we fished one out thinking there was treasure/ inside. There was. Dead treasure./ We were learning not to be so curious/ or romantic.* Quinton was reading the Italian poet and novelist Cesare Pavese at the time.

At his readings then, Quinton loved to laugh at his own expense and at the notion of poetry. "Scungilli" was one of his reading favorites—scungilli is sea snail, dense and rubbery, usually fried—*all our energy is suddenly assigned/ to swallow this wily conch in our mouths*…chewing because these are our words, this what we are given for a life, chewing *as if we were swallowing our tongues* until we must spit out what we can't consume.

Joe's Rain (2005) celebrates engagement. Rain as a concept in the title poem can be real rain and the punishing emotional spill in a friend's death. The random gifts of chance can rain down as well—on a curve in the roadway, a spill of cherries from the crates of the trucks delivering them. The poem moves from elegy to gratitude, the dominant note in the whole collection.

The consequences of events depend on how you read them—metaphor, the poet's way to talk about one thing in terms of another. *Let's compare events to things we feel,* the speaker says with a deliberate mix of elevated and cartoonish images in "Trying to Read Mythology," but concludes, *Maybe we should just shut up and eat.* Maybe there is an opportunity for transcendence or prayer, the speaker says in the delightful "Humble Pie," but maybe you just are on your knees, unable to find your dropped glasses, and that is the stance of a self-blinded incompetent not a saint.

His poems through the years show Quinton as he was—a person of such charm that he could afford to be wry in his ironies. The poems too are kind. Their artifice is so unassuming—just as an athlete instinctively knows economy of movement, or a painter knows how to frame a way of looking, Quinton knew syntactic development, knew where emotion swells and where it subsides. He was discriminating in his love for the indiscriminate (in one of his sidelines, he collected curios). His poems preserve the small minutes of things, the poetic perishables, and love itself is the chief item with its shine of frequent use illuminating so many of his poems.

—Dennis Schmitz

TABLE OF CONTENTS

OLTREMARINO

OUR TOWN

IN MEMORY OF BEING HAPPY

POSTSCRIPT

WHO IS NANCY LEE?

For all her penny brightness
in the gold spring morning
she rises, kisses the hem
of her day, humble, proud,
glad to be here again. I wish,
oh I wish I could be as glad
to greet each dawning day
as Nancy is glad. A celebration
plays inside her head and heart
and she walks with a jingle
on the tip of her pink tongue
about the new day, the day full
of opportunity, brimming with
possibility, with raw
material, and who's to know
what can be coaxed from it?

OLTREMARINO

Back Street Story

She fills the night with arias
as she brushes her hair in
the window with a full Florentine
moon beaming down on her, a full
moon dazzled by that hair
she brushes in long strokes
that fill the night air
with sparks. Light
from that moon and you
just stand there
wishing there was someone
with you to share the vision.
       But *you* are my reader forty-
five years later and the real other you
had already gone back to the hostel
to lie down after losing his
dinner in the piazza. You wonder
if you could live here, *parla Italiano*,
love this woman for as long as ever,
this woman who clearly loves another,
an *other* you can't imagine
doing anything not involving
grease and gas. Some *one* who
could not appreciate her combing,
her figure outlined by the moon,
the window song spilling from
her lips in silver coins that
bounce from the cobblestones
in front of you and disappear
like smoke into the dark
shadows where you stand
waiting for a life,

waiting for what you now know
has been your life, waiting
for a big finale—yes, with
all the players, and the stars,
the moon, the darkened street
a little off the square.

LONG DISTANCE

The perplexed, the fearful son
tries to connect long distance
to his mother's voice, water-like
rushing through the background
making everything said sound
weak and likely. He can imagine
red blood cells hurrying through her halls.
Is it anything like having your own
private bees? Pale bees who can't
find where the honey lies, that
wear themselves out looking?
Doctor, he needs some simple talk.
Speak a tongue unsweetened,
unstung by bees. Man, tell it
as it is, for him, for all of us
who loiter on the shores
of her life, losing the light,
snuffling in the wind, missing
the drift, the directions
to the distant waters.

AGENDA

September morning, outside
shirtless, in shorts and thinking
Picasso had shorts sort of
like mine. Marveling at the dawn-
purple of the tomatillos in my palm,
the paper husks pulled off,
the sticky little globes marked
with oceans and continents
and what a sour delicious core
those worlds reveal. Also,
I admire a still life of Early
Girls in their yellow dish
painted I'm sure by someone
before a late lunch outside Arles,
in the shade by a river.
Above the lovely sound of water
my wife cries, "Look at that!"
Praying Mantis moves drunk
across the glass table, prays
his way onto that red the Early Girls
give away for free. I half expect
the sawtooth jaws to begin to carve.
Nancy steers him to a leaf
then lifts him to the basil
where he seems pleased to light.
"The best revenge," this living
well, this using up a perfectly
good morning, then lunch
from the garden and a small nap
in the cool quiet of the house.

LUCK

Lucky am I to have crossed
the ocean in a liner, watched
yellow dozers cover a beached
whale with sand. I chant
the mantra of the coral
snake, whistle the uncertain
song of the meadowlark,
sing the call of local geese
that won't leave their cushy pond.
Lucky to have loved, in my way,
women who loved me back.
The golden age of love was back there
and we didn't even know it.
To read poems to a dying friend,
something, with luck, a friend will do
for me—poetry, anything stormy
and vibrating on the tongue:
a tornado washed a sky green
in Indiana;
a hurricane tore the steeple off
the church with God's howling wind;
an earthquake turned the swimming pool
into a small, wave-tossed sea.
Still, I come back to this harbor,
a room with table, lamp, window.
That river could be the Loire.
That sky could be the gray underside
of heaven. That rain, well,
that could be the world collecting
itself, a silver bullet in each drop.

LATE SUMMER

The subtle: how long the sun
bakes the west side of the house,
glaring inches a day, then losing
inches a day to shade. Shadows
flicker and breathe, elongate
to darker and darker closets of green.
How the tomatoes take on their color
and the chilies, picked green, turn
to red in the cool inside, at leisure.
I am sixty and changing too,
my dreams filled with sea-
water and flickering fires on some shore.
Remember summer in Oregon, how
fires opened like flowers down
the evening beaches? Sparks rose
into starry darkness. Now,
we never quite see the stars
in their true constellations clearly.
Conundrums abound. How the cat's summer
claw turns round into ram's horn, whorl
the curve's instinct allows. Horn worm ticks
on his green leaf, little chewing clock.
All things own the map to come home, to
change and sting—the subtle: as we are
unmoored, we are fastened
to the changing, growing light,
bidden to follow it through into ever-
lengthening shadow, the coming fall.

REACH FOR IT

Reach for it, the fallen star
burning a hole in the carpet,
the dime the fat man can't
quite pick up, the heart
that just won't give in
to your reaching finger.
Try to remember her lips
as if they were everything,
her hips and breasts,
the natural way she stood
naked and talked to you
as she felt the water warming.
The bath, the lowering,
the rising out of soapy foam
and water falling down her curves.
You're the one with the stories.
You can see the coal tracing
an ever-larger ring in the rug,
the spilled bourbon soaking into
your pants, the dime shining up
at you, knowing you can't make it
live in your pocket at your command.

The Coast at Cley

Students of art and nature, we were amazed
at how the sky, the sea, the rocky beach
could carry so much of the same color—
as if there weren't such elemental
differences in the age-old trio.
We knew that rocks were born
out of upheaval, grinding down, pressure
to fit the crescent of a boy's hand
when confronted with flat water.
We knew the pebbles in circles were
the nests of plovers who laid
careful eggs flecked with hues of stone.
The parents would burst away or
drag off dangling a wing in mock injury
while the eggs became stones with all
their might. If we looked up,
it wasn't because we understood
heaven's sky in all its grays,
and the line where it met the ocean
was only a point on the blackboard of art.
Of the sea, the moss-green frothing
its edges and bullied by the wind—
we were afraid. As if no boy
or girl ever got invited to stay,
as if time couldn't proceed
until the watery rooms filled with classes
of better scholars than us. No,
we'll cleave to the rock—on the beach,
in the concrete bunkers left over from the war,
in the composition of the road
as we cycled for home and the light
that changed each time we lifted our eyes.

Dogwood

How can you stay so beautiful?
At once so pale and broken
into blossoming scraps, then
the dark, smooth branches,
I mean black, that give up
an odd petal to the spring wind.

How do you seem to know
where to set yourself down?
You have all kinds of wild ideas.
I know redbud sees your play
of dark and light, and starts,
brushy, stubborn, with impossible seed.

All the right and fine things
derive from you, or something like you.
All the veined white blossoms
hold against the black branch, the alarm,
the thug of winter light, the whip
that arrives with such beauty.

My World

My world is a puzzle of places,
snapshots of my life, my town
collected from cities and towns
everywhere. There is a shale beach,
a wharf, a shabby boardwalk, a sea
chalked in by memory's hand,
any color from winter white to sunset
red and always the fractured, moving
water, breathing and heaving, alive.
My street, down which I move,
is cobble, my brother short-passing
my mother's pound of tea to my
receiving arms, running all the way
home. And home, a mixed-up
kitchen with a hungry, raging stove
and coal to be dragged in each day
to feed its gaping maw.
Yes, there is a chapel, and hymns
that tell stories from other times,
stories meant to praise God
but always God in *our* world
as if we are specially blessed.
We believe this, as we believe that
the hay rolled into those big loaves
is rolled for us, that the hillside
from which we count the clouds
as they trip over the mountain
and fall straight into our green valley
is where we live. That on
the hillside is where we go,
ashes or boxes, to see the rest.

MORNING LETTER

The teapot exhales its jet of steam—
the steam clouds drift and luff
with rising sun as backdrop.
Atlantic, where the sun begins.
You can't imagine an ocean
into which the sun does not slip.
Your Pacific, your left coast,
always the sunset, backdrop
to cocktail hour.
I don't know when
I've written you a letter
from the wrong side of myself.
You always liked my notes:
I wrote about a dog,
you said you could pet that dog;
I mentioned all this water,
and you said you could drink
the water from the page. Maybe
you are the poet, maybe
you just miss me
and my martyrdom here
on the right coast. I am hungry
for anything that smacks of you.
I cut lime for drinks, make
desultory dinner. I eat
what turns dry in the mouth—
crackers, bread with nothing
spread over it but sunlight.

Red Memory

How many times have you begun
"I was only a young man in those days,"
then laid the pen back down? Often
you can't recall
even the simplest version,
the grainy gray newsreel
of dazzling teeth, blood-red
lipstick darkened
with the years, certain eyes.

Were you a young man lost to looking
for love? You never knew
what you'd find, the difference
each time you stepped into the radiant
light of a lover, the perfume,
a texture, the very weather that entered
the small place where love was made
and traded. Clocks wandered
for those hours—*languid*
is the word that comes to your lips,
the lazy way she might have had
of raising her arm to unfurl
the curtain's pleat. A tongue
between teeth could last days.

Now memory returns, out of
the little hole she bored
and pushed a red thread through
to your side. You were sunk
as soon as you pulled it,
yards of red thread collecting
on your bed, the spinning bobbin

on the other side of the wall.
Even you, young man,
could not ignore those signs.
Recall your wild confusion when
you heard through the wall
the trappings of love and then
her inevitable sobbing, the soft white
throat of your possible lover
full of what you assumed was sorrow.
You discovered tears aren't always
sad. Some of us cry in joy, relief,
in the thin clear stream of music
the body gives willingly away
as it collapses, exhausted, into dust.

Bring back those short winter days
descending your step, ascending
her step, a hot bath, a clean bed,
wine in a cracked glass. It went on
until forever, until it was over,
end of story, chapter whatever,
you might have said once. No.
Now the curtain turns to rain,
Chevrolet, red exhaust in the
evening sky with attendant tears, your big
chest heaving, heaving, your hands
somehow waving the light away.

Success

Give away what power you possess,
power that makes you feel alone
until you send it away
with the last gold coin in your purse,
a kiss on the lips, and a map
of the good places to crash.
Once you picked up an angel
hitchhiking into town. He looked
like your brother around the eyes.
His wings were folded inside
a leather jacket with the name
of a hotel and a girl who lived there.
You gave him your cigarettes,
a couple of dollars and change.
You had the Olds, a woman
who said she loved you,
a room where silence snored
when you wanted to be alone.
Once, rain beat the leaky windows
and framed tall palms that wailed
in the wind. "What was *that*?"
you said out loud. A bird
you'd never seen flew into
the window and off again,
just a wet print on the glass.
All this you can spare. More even.
It's that water under the bridge
we talk about. It's waiting for us
to take the first drink.

POTATO SALAD

In a perfect world like this
it would come heaped
in grandmother's white bowl
down the back steps of this
little house in Elk Grove, or Oakdale,
or South Bend, or any other
optimistically named American town
that sprung out of the moxie
of people moving west toward
a new mystery of a century.
It's a world of smoke drifting
from the barbeque to the impossibly
blue sky of summer. Hot dogs
bark on the grill, the chatter of friends
telling wise and funny stories,
anticipating but never expecting
the potato salad to be delivered
by a pair of hands, a blue blouse
belonging to a face as stunning
in its beauty as any face ever beheld.
And those white shorts, white
as clouds, and the long sun-
tanned legs that reach all the way
down to the perfect surface
of the back yard.

OUR STORY

As we lie in bed together
you remove a veil, tell me
you weren't supposed to be born,
the doctor having ruled out
another child for your mother.
Yet here you are—named, baptized,
fed and watered, full-size, *here*.

You were born on a morning full
of March fog, a mantilla
of caul shrouding your red face
and a song in your throat.
Your eyes are still
blue as they were that day.
I'm sure small clouds crossed them
as they took note of the bright world.
The nurse bathed your flaming
6 lb.- 4¼ oz. body, first baby
born that Monday morning.

As I lie in bed *this* Monday,
watching you rise to bathe
before work, I see no path
that led you to my door, no
theme as you begin to hum
over the rush of the shower.
I can't tell how our story
will end, this ordinary homage
to everyday love, but the days arrive
bearing news of the world created
the day you were born,
the moment we met, every time
we wave goodbye.

WATERCOLOR SKETCH

The broken line along sea and sand
then, higher, sea and horizon.
A boat defaces planes of light
and water with red snapping sails,
metal banged by rope. Wail
of noon whistle across the bay,
mournful as a baby left asleep
in the shade of an olive tree
for gypsies to raise.
Red sails are just chambers,
a heart full of love for you.
We drift toward the opposite shore
where sea meets sky, horizon.
Man the tiller or meet the rocks,
the old men say. We take turns
steering, blind, lying on the ribs,
looking up to learn the curve of
heaven from a moving boat.

LIE STILL

I say let the corpse dance. Make the living lie still.
—Richard Hugo

There is morning light
that saturates the doorway
and we are home in a house
I've never been. Mother
looks well, rested and bright,
surprised that *we* are surprised,
we who touch her and turn
to each other—you see her too?
The yellow light burns joyous
and we all weep. Brothers,
and a sister, we are all here.
Even Dad drops in, young,
suit and tie, reading specs.
He stays quiet, happy to arrive.
"Mother, how can you do this?"
I ask. *"My* mother visited about
four times a year," she smiles.
"You never told anyone? You
never said?" She has to go
and we are alone, children
of this mother and father, we
who survive. My sister and I
hold each other as the furies
begin their parade. I think
we are supposed to know
what they can do if they want to.
Even in all the buttery light
there are blackbirds waiting to fly.

Man Driving

Driving south, he feels his foot
rise and fall on the pedal.
His fingers wrap the wheel—
is there enough room for blood,
he grips so tight?
He likes this road, a real road,
trees on either side
that lean in to touch
high in the canopy. Fields,
either side alfalfa new-mown
or rows of sugar beets,
safflower massed together.
The point is how the road
cuts through them in a ruler-
straight line to the end.
Other cars pass, turn off,
blinkers far ahead or behind.
Pickups outside the diner,
he's tired but doesn't stop.
There is a limit to this line,
this road, there is a place
where it will turn away.
His foot rises and falls. Water
turns silver in the furrows
as dusk descends. He can smell
the water, the wet soil, the heat
still rising from the blacktop.
No one knows anything, not
the owl flashed in the lights,
not the coyote out for a jog,
not the roadside shrine with
its all-weather flowers, not
this man, this wide-open,
unsteady, driving man.

Human Anatomy

Stripped to muscle and sinew, bone,
shown in pose convenient to the student,
the man just looks lonely. No one else
lives in his world. No man or woman
to say his name, put smoky fingers
between his teeth and fill him
with something called love.
He sees no other eyes staring back
into his, eyes that see animal
and man shapes in the stars, eyes
that close alone. He must have come
from somewhere he decides, and even
deciding feels lonely when no other
nods his head, holds his arm erect
and moves his hand like a bird's wing.
He knows not where he travels, nor why
he treks alone. He lives well before
God takes over, blesses the animals
and shames mankind. He walks an earth
with no rules except to live until he stops,
and the hollow chest he carries is for something
yet to be rendered.

EARLY REPORT

The motor of your breathing
is precise, regular as any dream
wrapped in the stiff, starchy sheets
and hotel blanket.

A gull, blood-splashed beak cocked,
alights on the ledge, full of fish
and trash the sea offers as waves
keep peddling their story.

My heart dives into the haze,
blue and silver when it reappears.
Our story washes up here, vague
on the edge, blue, silver, salty.

Who will read our life together
in its foreign tongue years
from now? The future, after all,
is what comes after us.

OLTREMARINO

And as the rain fell down, silver
dropped from the corrugated tin
roof edge, but there was no blue
to be had in any direction. "Degrees
of gray," the poet said—hung over
the sea, curtains on November's stage.
Last night we heard geese battling
their way through the storm
while satellite weather showed a mass
of rain and wind come from across the sea,
(the *Pacific*, of all seas) sweeping east
to draw its veil over our house.
It was weather, just one more thing
to wash color from our lives.
I was blue and I don't know what
you were singing. In the gray
I tried not to show it, my cobalt blush
hidden in the dark. I felt I was from over
the sea—*oltremarino*—if that is blue,
if that is a feeling at all. Alien
is one word for it—out of place and time—
wishing to go into the gray like those geese,
to wash clean in the weather, flying
by instinct and taut to the group
of strangers I travel with, all of us heading
to the place of instinct, the reeds,
among islands that await our raucous calling.

OUR TOWN

*EMILY: Do any human beings ever realize life
while they live it?—every, every minute?*

*STAGE MANAGER: No. . . . The saints and poets,
maybe—they do some.*

I. Our Town

Our town is somewhere out there.
Tourists wander down our streets
lost in fog, question marks
above their heads.
Old man bluejay sits on a bench
in front of the deli, acting out
the story of his days in flight.
He used to be so good—
you could hardly see the wire.
He'd pose, cigarette in hand,
as if he and God were friends.
You may not know this
but I, too, used to be someone
well thought of, sought out
for advice. I'm not sure
why people listened to me.
I tried to tell the truth. I tried
to call a cloud a cloud
and when it rained, quick I'd say *rain*,
so there was always a reason for rain.

II. The Stranger

Open with the young vagabond
coming toward us, a black dot
that gradually forms arms, legs,
a head, then features and colors
emerge, as if distance is fog and
closer is clear air. We can read
his face: he comes from over there,
where the devil is in the driver's seat.
He doesn't know that "over there"
is everywhere, that horror
moves faster than any imagination.
He carries a bundle into which
he has tied his book, his razor,
a picture of his family eating
together outside under a plane tree.
That is the dash of nostalgia.
Also, he carries a small dog with
eyes like carved coal. Tucked
under his jacket, the dog represents
hope. The ending will surprise us.
We don't know what happens next,
only that it will be sad, and the hero
is the hero because of this.

III. Mariner

I washed ashore like Moses,
belly full of sea water,
ears full of kelp—no wonder
the song of the ocean plays
in the halls of my hollow head.
My bed was a biscuit box
by the stove in the rigging store.
I could speak in tongues—
Spanish, Portuguese, English—
before I was dry. I saw worlds
through the grate of the stove,
each lump of coal glowing
like dawn before the storm.
I took my comfort on water
but I always came back
where the sea set me down
those many years ago. This town
is mine, and even out of the corner
of my eye, everything is in place
for me here at the edge, one man
rising and falling with the tide.

IV. The Aviator

I arrived by air, by the light
of a million stars. The radium dial
on my watch burned 11:47
as the silk parachute lowered
me to the silver grass.
I came down hard, but I lay still
as the silk fluttered in the starlight
and down the valley flames rose
from the burning plane. Torches
wound toward me up the hill
away from the slumbering town.
Could I still speak a tongue
they would understand? I tried
to sing a solstice song but my heart
had wandered out of sight.
The rest is unclear until I opened
my eyes one morning and cried
in my thin gown like a newborn.
So I became a citizen of second chances.
I made a life here out of spit and wire,
and it works like a dream.

V. Orphan

Gulls tune their flutes.
In the woodwind fog, bass chug
of boats coming home replete
with silver anchovy, anxious
to pump this sluice
into cannery tanks. Waterfront
laid hard against the frothy,
lightening sea. Twice daily, ferry
slides in to dock, gangplank,
people madly waving.
Fishermen brave the jetty spray
to cast out where the deep rock
fish lie in wait for hooked mussels—
perch and cabezon waving
in the current's breeze. Going away
is long term for us. Always
leaving, we might never know
who made us, who gave us up.
"Ain't got no muddah, ain't got no faddah,"
the song goes. Do my parents rest
at the bottom of the sea, or with earth
mounded up around them? Do they
sleep on the hill above the town
among the yellow broom and ivy?
There is a room in my heart
where no one has ever slept. Someday
the key will be gone from its nail
when I get home. People I recognize
will be waiting to explain.

VI. THE DROVER

He doesn't give a damn
about what we think is beautiful.
Not the view off south
where the river winds like silver
through the valley.
Not the way clouds back up
against the green spring hills.
He sees all he wants
when the breeze blows over
the bull's loose hide. We might
compare it to wind combing
a small field of red wheat.
He loves the bulls, the smell
of bulls, the power that lives
under their thick hide. At night
by the fire, he knows things
have been true since man first stood
still long enough to herd. Outside
the shape of light the fire builds,
the animals nuzzle each other,
digest the darkness slowly, aware
of the sentry dog. The drover falls
asleep among the simple shapes
grazing in pale moonlight.

VII. Odd Man

Children like me
but their mothers are afraid.
Animals like me.
They understand that
some people live
a simple life.
What could be more
simple than fire, water, air?
I have a house with two windows
and a door that opens
to any friend. I keep a fire
in my stove. I work for food,
clothes, gather the rest.
I own one red rowboat
and a pair of green oars.
You have seen me rowing
out beyond the jetty to keep
the ferry company. Gulls
wheel over my head
and make a joyful noise,
angels singing different songs
all at once. When I die
they'll follow me rowing
out to the sun singing
their squawky tunes
as I rise to join them.

VIII. THE SHEPHERD

I wanted more and more sky
so I walked—blanket, pan, dog—
to the top of the world. I came alone
with eight hundred friends, what you call
sheep, and a trillion stars.
Town is a glow in the night, north about
eleven o'clock. Night, when this world
begins its singing. My little guitar
can't match the music of wind and stars
and grass talking in its sleep. I sing
of frosted evenings split by the coyote's wail,
campfire smoke and stars dropping
through space behind the dark horizon.
I wanted to be alone, to feel closer
to another place up here so high.
A child could draw my life: tree, wagon,
bed, dog, fire. I am the stick man
bending to the wind. You can see the notes
escape my mouth under that moon
that resembles a white comma.
By the fire of crossed stick-lines, the simple dog,
dazzled alert by the collective moaning
of the flock, joins the chorus with his bark.

IX. Gardener

My good fortune was to come here
where two rivers meet, and the sea loiters
outside the harbor, waiting to begin.
First, I was drawn to sea, and I lived
for years with water under my keel.
Then I came ashore for good
and buried my hands in the earth,
as if my long white fingers would sprout
themselves. As if the whole world
and its cruelties, anemic and pale,
could be persuaded into the white
flesh of these potatoes I grew,
for a little water and a soupspoon
of faith. I began to sing in the evening
and the plants joined in. Their green
tongues flapped in the wind,
but I understood. All my years at
sea, and the sea only mumbled
when I cried my young eyes out
over love and the shape of a heart!
It was the constant garden taught me
of women, the private things I dream,
of green and fresh water pushing into salt.
It comes together thus: your hands
get dirty, you wash them clean.
There is no stain left to anguish,
no one to mourn. You can sing,
you can sing. Sad and joyous,
the plot awaits.

X. The Teacher

I walked the shore daily
when I was young, sky draped
in gray muslin or sun vaulting
off water. I was there, pockets
filled with shells and stones, worn
glass and bits of crockery.
When I met my poet, we joined,
a twosome on the shore, and he
would write of "the solitary bird"
and "the belt of winter weed" lying
in a reeling dark band offshore.
Our secret speech was in cadence
with the pulse of waves. Even in starlight,
firelight, the waves. We wed,
built a little cabin on dunes above
the bay. In time for war to come
calling, and my poet went to war,
died aboard his sweeper, a German
U-boat in the North Sea. I imagine
him, my solitary bird, each day
as I walk the arc of beach.
For years I brought my students here,
taught the sea and its secrets, its leavings
as a subject worth study, read the poems
that the poet left, that others left.
Plover eggs in circles of stones,
flecked and speckled like gravel,
my love lives under the sea, and I will
walk the edge until my time to go
deeper into the mystery, go under
the cover of water. I imagine
a beach ready for walking,
someone, it could be him, to walk with.
Someone for whom salt water means
the world, from which a new world begins.

XI. The Old Man

We remember the old man stepping out
of a book, his hands moving,
his eyes the color of washed blue cotton.
He believed in work, and God
in what he could see—
the clouds, the hills, the water.
He snared birds with a wire loop,
cooked them over his fire.
He gathered honey, caught fish,
drank rainwater when he could,
traded for wine, oil, salt.
Hot days he slept afternoons,
wandered nights lost and joyful
under stars that hung above
in their silver sockets.
There were women over the years,
but his life was lonely, and God
isn't simple for most of us.
He played music that no one knew,
danced his own step, flew off
one day when no one was looking.
He is not an owl or a hawk.
We don't know what he is now.

XII. Testament

I began to see my days marked
up to the mystery. Clouds
that gathered and dispersed
on the crooked line of the mountains
were the future: always there.
I did what anyone might do
to feed and clothe myself—
so help me God I followed my soul.
If it said, "Learn music
you can carry with you," I found
the mouth harp and began to compose.
I never knew I had music
inside me, waiting like that.
Music led me to women, and I learned
as much as I could, that no man
can learn much about women,
their hills and valleys, shadows, clouds
and rain. I was in awe of
the heavens, above us and inside us.
Look at me suddenly getting plural
when I was so often alone.
I said an unpracticed goodbye.
Clouds and rain on the tips
of mountains prodding the sky,
music pouring from some well,
I stepped into the light.

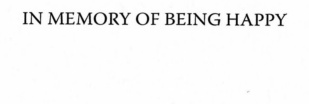
IN MEMORY OF BEING HAPPY

SPOON

for Paul Zarzyski

There was one in my father's tackle box,
your father had one too,
that could have been stamped and rolled
from a silver dollar but was nothing
so rare—sheet metal and chrome.
I loved the three ruby beads
threaded on the stiff connecting wire
and the little gold propeller, a kick
to imagine it calling out to the lunkers.

But it was the hook, welded on edge,
dangerous, that thrilled the boy, the barb
poised, benign, to pierce the white lip
of the fish, hold him as he's hauled
through the green ceiling of his world.

There were so many things to name
back then, in the rainclouds, the boat
drifting on the early morning
lake, your father's coffee and cigarettes,
fried egg sandwiches in waxed paper
waiting for lunch. We chose words,
to love them, to put them next to each other—
fish on the stringer we might
or might not bring back to the cabin, grinning
like the simple fools we still are.

How many years will we still pull words
from the inside, fish bones, yes, and round tones
ringing like campfires in the crisp air?
We can't forget all this, even when our voices

play tricks on us, haul us wet and terrified
into new worlds. We will gasp and love
the sound of gasping. We will turn
silver and glisten.

GEESE

Gauguin's watercolor reveals two geese
among weeds, four goslings playing: *Geese
and Goslings, 19th Century.* They make noise
I know by heart in this 21st century having
battled geese myself, on occasion, having
had a father who owned a gander stick,
having had a friend with geese, and a car
with attractive chrome and rubber trim his geese
removed out of boredom and cussedness.
Memory allows their noise to become music,
Julian Bream's Spanish guitar in this case.
And geese lead to remembering that sudden
shadow across the yard, and the outcry
as hawk hit chicken, its limp neck and last
twitching as it rose into the morning sky.
Soundtrack by Bream and the spawn creek
behind the cabin, spongy meditation deck—
who could concentrate on one's inner space when
outside, the salmon, fins breaking water, pushed
up creek home? Remember the music, the food, the dope,
the cheap gas and junk cars, friendship, love, moonlight,
firelight, cold water, goats, geese, wine, poetry, liberty,
happiness, when we were still too far from the end
to see it turn to history.

ONE BRIGHT MORNING

for Loren Chandler, 1937-2006

Freeway traffic was stopped dead
so I followed the river road.
Hay trucks crawled south to Ryer Island
as balers in the fields pulled drying
alfalfa into the front end and dumped out
fresh bales behind. West, Mount Diablo,
then the Delta spread before me,
the Delta you loved to the end.
It was a glorious morning, and I stopped
to take a memorial piss in the snakegrass
and salute the breeze riffling the water's
blue skin. A man dropped traps
along the slough. I found myself taking
the crawdad's side—no traps!—all quarry
left behind. I couldn't see anything
detained on a morning like this.
The landscape gathered into our last trip—
sheep with new lambs, Canadian geese, Great
Blue Heron climbing the air like old men.
Last time I saw you, sinking into your bed,
it was morning, bright, promise of noonday heat.
Hours after I was gone, you were gone.
Simple as that. "One bright morning,"
goes the song, "I'll fly away."
Forgive the hymn, friend. Out of doors
it doesn't count as praying.

SURPRISE

The faces in the cancer ward fit
lives you've known or dreamed.
Impossible, but there they are,
grape-stained collars and age-spotted
hands that grow more familiar
with each breath and beat of your heart.

You were going to say *racing heart*
as your heart used to race when,
walking through the woods,
you'd be attending something
to the side and wander
into a spider's web that wrapped
your face and blurred your vision.
And you prayed you saw, through the scrim
over your eyes, the black and yellow
spider's retreat. Surprise!

Oh, the times you've looked up
to see what you did not pray for
or held the telephone in broad daylight
to hear the doctor's foreign tongue, the voice
of doom to the seventh power: "You'll live
but you won't be able to dance
any better than you ever could."

So when you gather the courage
to look up, to answer the phone,
to open the brown paper bag to see
what lurks in your lunch today,
and it's white bread, yellow cheese, and salve,
you take a little bite and—surprise—
you like it, goddamn it, you like it.

In Memory of Being Happy

October evening, darkness
settles early now. Moon
is a candle lit for those
who wander, take the world
as a map and read its
surface as the skin
of a lover we knew.
How we traced hills and valleys
and the distance between.
Remember the white daubs of dotted
swiss rushing to the floor, ankles
stepping out into charged air—
Here we are, and what are you
going to do about it? *Plenty*,
the saying goes. And imagine
the time we squandered
on each other, the raw lips
and fingers we offered
again and again. Moon,
there's the moon, lover.
Goodbye, into this darkness
we walk as if we've lost our lifeline.

OCEANIC

In the breeze, I sometimes smell the sea,
her salty funk all night
dancing around beach fires and
the trip in over lowlands—
swamp and slough water
in her nostrils. East, North,
she lays her skirts about her
and her voice grows soft
as a lover's, inland, where
the river tightens and even
the salmon come to streams
too small to proceed. She lies
back—picnic basket, blanket under
cottonwood, a day when clouds slow
to see her shining there. Good Lord,
thank you for the chicken, the cold
wine, the river coming down from
its source. Thank you for lips, a tongue,
and some imagination. For finger-
tips and skin warmed by sunlight.
Thank you for the sea, for what the river
discovers at its end, what waits
for all of us to come calling.

RED HAIR

At dawn, a milk blue arm points out
a mass of flame on the pillow.
There is no need to fly away
from such a storm as this.
This is no need like seeing.
To the shadow, dark as smoke,
to the nightgown, white as soap,
to the coffee on the stove.
To the new day, the mockingbird,
a month closer to fall, and to all
the small fires the red leaves will supply.
Bless her eyes, she'll wake
and find me out. Surely,
I can water, throw feed at the stock,
and be back before this is all gone.
I hope she's dreaming about a good life,
a life with me in charge of mornings,
of smoke-filled days in fall when I can't
believe the fires. Of ordinary days,
after all, decorated by this need.

What's Left

Who can expect life
will hold on shyly for years
in a bleak, gray bed
and threaten to let go
but never quite get to it?
God in his wisdom allows
the giving up, the grief, the truth.
What flowers can be saved
when the wind makes its thorough
ravishing complete?
All blown apart, we say,
stripped of raiment and shivering
in the interloping season.

Matins—October

How the dust rises up
on the horizon, fills the air
from below. How the color
is like some bruise, smoke
but not from fire.
This is earth and air together.
No wonder we are excited.
No wonder we see the way
wind can move earth
from place to place, settle
a fine ground layer
on almost anything.
How the sun works its light
through the veil. And birds
sing all the while. We watch
a vee of geese fly right
into the cloud of dust off
to the south, determined to go
south when something tells them
to go. We lift our eyes to the noise,
we salute their passing,
try to count but lose track.
Looking into the pool, I was trying
to fish out leaves the wind had left
when I first saw their vee reflected,
and then I heard their cries.
Then, before I turned to tell you,
I saw my face looking back
and I wasn't sure at all
if the look on my face was surprise
the geese brought, or shock
to meet myself in that water.

Café Society

It's not autumn or summer,
but in between, and here
under these plane trees
at these small green tables,
a breeze comes wandering through
and people seem happy
to sit and nurse their thoughts.
One child, not old enough to know,
forms an O with fruit-stained lips
and howls a great howl.
As if on cue, the boy's mouth,
the size of a wineglass
of local red wine, stops crying
and begins to mimic the town band.
Amazingly, what has struck the child
turns out to be the town band
tuning up for an evening wedding
mingled with the chuffle
of gathering blackbirds high above us.
I consider my wine, half gone,
my third. Then, against the lowering
sun, dinner plates rise up through the leaves
as if suddenly eager to fly.
Again, the scene takes a moment,
and what were plates become, sensibly,
white wedding balloons escaping the caterer.
"Here comes the wine!" I sing
to the tune of "Here Comes The Bride."
I am giving in. The pea gravel under
my shoes could be the dimpled skin
of a sleeping beast. To the beast!
The air is thick as wine. To air!
To spotted hands, to the tongue twisted
until it squalls like a little boy.

Cough Cough

Sometimes the water goes down wrong,
down your "Sunday throat," your wife says.
It takes no genius to bring up
death, it occurs to you as your face turns
the blue of skimmed milk, then
bullfrog blue in the offensive
sparkly, lack-of-oxygen high.
When you can breathe again, hallelujah,
hot water runnels through
your sinuses and out your nose,
thank you. Head clears, blood
pressure falls back from the brink
and the mercury shining in your eyes
shrinks back into the sacs until next time
when it runs out once and for all
and lays those little Xs down on
your pupils, the signal, the beacon,
the international sign for *gone, daddy-o.*

LONELY VISTAS

Sometimes the longing begins early,
mornings steering the tractor through
uniform lines of grapes. The mist
settles between the rows, down where
the sulphur grabs hold of the leaves
and workers get that little cough
and surprising yellow in the kerchief.
But you are riding higher, inside the cab
no outer noise can seep into.
Bored, you decide the noise of the motor
is the noise it takes to make the whole
dark engine run, what it costs to play.
And all you see are unchanging rows,
occasional returns, like a ship
on a stage, afloat by simple optical
illusion. What others would see
as lucky, you write off as lonely
vistas, the same old same old thing.
Today you had bologna in your sandwich.
Today is Thursday. You can't remember
if that's what Thursdays always bring.
You long for a highway, a free-for-all
white line of constant change. The hands
that fold the lunch meat, lubricate the bread,
are hands you have watched for years.
Are they yours or hers? Does she wonder
where those lonely vistas will lead you?
Does she know how separate we are?

WASHLINE

The sun is twice as bright
against the bleached load
of sheets, towels, and things
I'm hanging on the line.
I try to imagine what goes next
to what. I give myself over
to the damp little blouse
like a cloud with the air let out.
I hang it next to my shirt
and feel form come back to me
as I touch your absent back
so startling in the blank sun.
I hang the panties in a row
like a stringer of little perch.
A few minutes ago these pale things
all swam together in the washer's tub.
Now, as I finish, they flap
in the hot wind, stiffening,
gaining a voice, coming into focus
cleanly against the cry
of the insisting jay. In counterpoint
to far off traffic, they return
to what they are, relaxing,
though pinned against a sky
that holds only, above the treetops,
a little plane whining off west.

Memory Leaves Me

Everything happened so long ago.
Show me one photo of my young face
smiling in front of snow-capped peaks
and I'm booked for the flight.
I remember those glasses I'm wearing,
the ones that fell off my face
and into a pond in Spain,
and how I put my arms into that green
water and groped, imagining another
month in Europe, wandering blind,
hands in supplication. I reclaim
that jacket, how the down kept coming
out of the seams. I molted for a year
and gave it up. What good am I
now, with these tips on how to live
a life: be careful, you could go blind,
lose your stuffing, even *die*.
It *has* been a long time. Memory
rearranges itself and I become
third person, not myself,
and because I am a guy who reads,
the story begins again, and this time
I can even fix what's coming. History,
mine anyway, always needs a smoke break
at this point. Why not relax, let it
become another story, not a best-seller,
just something to reread when rain
ruins an afternoon.

The Fabulous Future

My mother sits on her stool
at the sink, peeling carrots
and potatoes. Here she sits
washing dishes, making a drink,
talking on the phone. I see her
when I make my weekly phone call
and it gives me some comfort
to remember her thus.

She has a little platform
suspended on cable that lowers
and raises one story through
the deck on which she places
her day's gatherings and runs them up,
or, say, loads laundry for the trip down.
The winch motor screams in the forest,
but it's a question of practical
versus peaceful.

Maybe the future will be peaceful,
a lot of it, occasionally shattered
by the grinding of the winch. The birds
will stop their small racket for a time
and then pick up again.
The creek will swell, and then relax.
And the rain. My mother always tells me
if there is rain, or sun, or wind, if
she has opened the windows, if she has
had to light a fire.

Well, there will be rain, and rain brings
green to the leaves, fat to the lean
belly of the creek. And left alone,
the ivy will cover everything in time.

TIME'S ARROW

I was in awe of the face
looking back from the snapshot
your surprise letter held:
"Me—2002." And it *is* you,
your eyes the most articulate,
still the blank challenge, full-open
in a face that has evolved.

I would expect that with anyone,
but you are framed in my heart,
if I may say that: "You—circa 1982."
We knew what we were making
became the past as soon as it left
one set of lips for the other.
We breathed in each other's words
and saved them away like cordwood
for fires when we would be alone.

Maybe it's just me, the foot-dragger,
the forestaller. Do you feel time's arrow
work its way out the other side
of you too? Your letter is as light
as ether. If your picture caught fire
I would inhale the familiar smoke.

Your hands and your hair,
your belly and your long back,
your eyes spilling tears of joy
sometimes, others not. Talk about
how the years fall upon us. Time's
whole quiver seems empty now.

Like Hay

They smell like hay to me,
your last sweet words
blown across the fields
of the bedroom and out
the window to join the real breeze
moving the trees and changing
May light from green to gold.
There is no more hair to braid,
to keep wound in linen,
lain among the folds of sheets, sheets.
The soft release of air,
final vague sound of some word—
what was it going to be—
the secret of the other side?
(Oh, so this is what it is to die!)
If the smell is hay, newly mown,
we'll be all right. We'll make it
our anthem, our last sweet breath close
to a window ledge on a late spring day.

Album

Prokofiev sits in his study,
on one album cover, relaxed
in an armchair, tie and tweed
jacket. Two fingers that can play
anything hold a cigarette, idly
I can tell, as he dreams or thinks
of anything but the photographer
who works on making a portrait
of the master sitting idly, thinking
up melodies or note clusters
or whatever he thinks about.
I think about the blue smoke
of the cigarette in the afternoon
light. I like the idea of smoke
and light in the portrait.
I like the folded handkerchief
in his breast pocket.
I have spent a lifetime
in the wilderness of my own reflection.
That boy, that man, that old, fat man
won't look at me watching him.
I try to face forward, so the print
won't reveal my depth, my habit
of opening my mouth for the lens.
I want the smoky study in blues and grays.
I want to know who the guy in my pictures
thinks he is, and why he's snapping me.

OLD FRIEND

How is it for you, alone
so much of your life? Time is different
for all of us solitary travelers.
Here the days snap together seamlessly
and the hours grow frightening for their length.
Do you remember summer on the lake,
those long, slow days when we lay
in the bottom of the boat and the sky
was a boat-shaped blue? We imagined
we could complete this life in that sky-boat.
I didn't know the drifting never ceases.
Here I am, still adrift, still marking
the minutes' progress. Memory is my crew.
I practice every day being still,
waiting for the silence to end. One day
I might come to visit. Watch
for a boat on the horizon, your old friend
waving through the haze. If you could only
light the lantern, stoke the beach fire,
shout hosannas as the boat comes in.

Morning Tea

What the leaves arrange in the cup
could be constellation, profile of the poet,
map of the last leg of the journey.
We are heading towards somewhere
with a view, above a little town
where we'll receive mail and buy
three-day-old papers to read.
The café is almost always open.
Of course there's a bar—every café has
a bar. One good restaurant next door
cooks fish that swam this morning
in the sea we bid daily
Hello and Goodbye. One day
I suppose we won't be together.
You'll come to find me still in bed,
eyes like that fish we ate last night
mooning at the trip already begun.
Before I left, I saw you set out
the blue bowl full of speckled eggs
and a plate of June peaches.
After breakfast, find Bobo the fisherman
and his four sons. Tell them to bring rope
and a sheet of plywood. I've never had
a ride on plywood. I've never loved anywhere
as much as here, with you. I'd do it again
in a minute. You know me.
I've never had enough.

POSTSCRIPT

Valentine

The paper says two tawny frog-mouths
at the zoo found each other
late in life. I don't know
what a tawny frog-mouth is
but I swear that grainy photo
is you and me talking
about the future or the past,
it doesn't matter. You are there,
part of everything I see,
every fractured sunset,
every bleached bone of driftwood
that lands upon our shore.
Hold my hand and walk with me—
I'm still your pirate—as we part
the foam that wind scatters,
and leave our footprints behind
to fill with brine and disappear.

NOTES

"Agenda"—"Living well is the best revenge" is often ascribed to Gerald Murphy and is the title of a memoir about Gerald and Sara by Calvin Tomkins. The line is actually taken from George Herbert's collection of outlandish proverbs, 1630.

"Red Memory"—"I was only a young man/ In those days" is from James Wright's "Hook."

"Potato Salad"—original epigraph: OMG
                              NW IV TASTD EVYTHNG
                              IM N HVN
                              OMG
                              NW I CN DI

"Lie Still"—the epigraph is from Richard Hugo's "The Right Madness on Skye."

"Oltremarino"—"Degrees of Gray in Philipsburg" by Richard Hugo.

OUR TOWN—the epigraph is from Act III of Thornton Wilder's *Our Town*.